BIG BU$INE$$

Virgin

Adam Sutherland

First published in 2014 by Wayland
Copyright © Wayland 2014

Wayland
338 Euston Road
London NW1 3BH

Wayland Australia
Level 17/207 Kent Street
Sydney, NSW 2000

Commissioning editor: Annabel Stones
Designer: LittleRedAnt (Anthony Hannant)
Picture researcher: Shelley Noronha

ISBN: 978 0 7502 8065 5

Dewey categorisation: 338.7'61-dc23

Printed in Malaysia

10 9 8 7 6 5 4 3 2 1

Wayland is a division of Hachette Children's Books, an Hachette UK company.
www.hachette.co.uk

Picture acknowledgements: The author and publisher would like to thank the following for allowing their pictures to be reproduced in this publication: Cover: Getty Images; p.4: AFP/Getty Images; p.5: LFI/Photoshot; p.6: Brian Moody/REX; p.7: Gamma-Rapho/Getty Images; p.8: Michael Ochs Archives/Getty Images; p.9: Denize Alain/Corbis KIPA; p.10: Warner Bros/Everett collection/Rex; p.11: John Alex Maguire/REX; p.12: Chris Parypa Photography/Shutterstock.com; p.13: Bloomberg/ Getty Images; p.14: Featureflash/Shutterstock.com; p.15 top: wcjohnston/istockphoto; p.15 bottom: cdwheatley/istockphoto; p.16: Mike Kemp/In Pictures/Corbis; p.17: Getty Images; p.18: Fernando Cortes/Shutterstock; p.19: Nils Jorgensen/REX; p.20: Richard Baker Farnborough/Alamy; p.21: Picture Alliance/Photoshot; p.22 bottom: Ben Stansall/REX; p.22 top: s_bukley/Shutterstock.com; p.24 & title page: Jon Hrusa/epa/Corbis; p.25: Helga Esteb/Shutterstock.com; p.26: Photoshot; p.27: Featureflash/Shutterstock.com.

Contents

We have lift off!

Think of Virgin and what comes to mind? Banking, music, trains, air travel, home entertainment, mobile telephones... the list goes on and on. As a collection of more than 400 companies worldwide, the Virgin Group had revenues of £15 billion in 2012.

Virgin Chairman Richard Branson started his first business in 1968 at the age of just 16. Forty-five years later, he announced Virgin's next great adventure – space tourism. Like a lot of Virgin companies, there is solid business sense behind Virgin Galactic, as well as Richard Branson's well-known mix of adventure and fun. A company that can provide sub-orbital space travel, and manufacture the space craft to make it happen, could easily become one of the most profitable companies in the world!

Richard Branson at the opening of Spaceport America in New Mexico, home to Virgin Galactic.

4

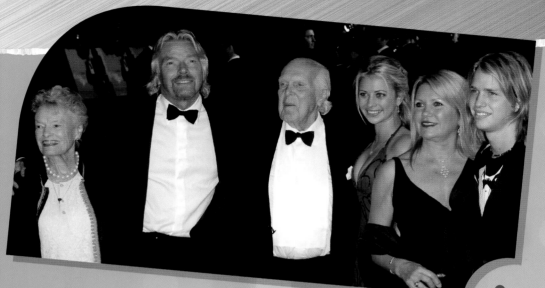

Branson and family at the premiere of Casino Royale.

The first Virgin Galactic flight is expected to take place in early 2014 – with Branson and his family on board! Reality show producer Mark Burnett, the creator of worldwide TV hits *Survivor*, *I'm A Celebrity, Get Me Out Of Here* and *The Voice*, has partnered with Virgin to create a reality show called *The Space Race*, where contestants compete for a ticket into orbit.

The Virgin story is a fascinating journey from school dorm room, through recording studios, airports, gyms and living rooms to outer space. How did a young man with dyslexia who left school at 16 with few qualifications, become one of the world's most successful and well respected businessmen? Read on to find out.

The Virgin Group: how it all works

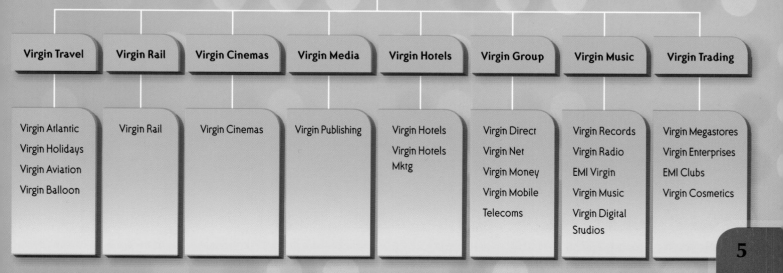

Virgin Travel	Virgin Rail	Virgin Cinemas	Virgin Media	Virgin Hotels	Virgin Group	Virgin Music	Virgin Trading
Virgin Atlantic	Virgin Rail	Virgin Cinemas	Virgin Publishing	Virgin Hotels	Virgin Direct	Virgin Records	Virgin Megastores
Virgin Holidays				Virgin Hotels Mktg	Virgin Net	Virgin Radio	Virgin Enterprises
Virgin Aviation					Virgin Money	EMI Virgin	EMI Clubs
Virgin Balloon					Virgin Mobile Telecoms	Virgin Music	Virgin Cosmetics
						Virgin Digital Studios	

Music by mail

Some businesses spring from a single invention, or a specific idea – like Facebook or Google – but many more grow from the entrepreneurial spirit of their founders. Virgin founder Richard Branson took his first steps into business while still in his teens.

At just 16 years old, Branson left school to launch a magazine called *Student*. When the first issue was published, his ex-headmaster said, 'Congratulations, Branson. I predict you will either go to prison or become a millionaire.' The young entrepreneur would eventually do both.

Student covered literary greats like Jean-Paul Sartre, Alice Walker and poet Robert Graves – but never made any money. However, spurred on by his music-loving friends, Branson hit on the idea of importing records and selling them at discount prices by mail order, using the magazine to run ads for the new business.

Virgin Mail Order – the first building block in Virgin's eventually global empire – almost started life as Slipped Disc. But Tessa Watts, one of the *Student's* staff, pointed out that they were all 'complete virgins at business' and the new name stuck.

The mail order business was quickly earning more than the magazine. Encouraged by its success, Branson rented a space above a shoe shop on Oxford Street in London, and the first Virgin Record Shop was born.

> I knew very little about the record industry, but from what I saw at the record shop… the real potential for making money lay in the record companies.

Richard Branson, Losing My Virginity, 1998

A young Branson working on Student magazine – his first business – in 1968.

Branson opens a Virgin Megastore in Berlin, Germany – the brand spread worldwide.

Branson worked behind the counter and sold the first LP himself. Another store followed in Liverpool, and then 12 more around the country. They became cool places for young people to hang out, and challenged the dominance of established – but 'square' – high street stores like WH Smith.

However, Virgin was soon in trouble with HM Customs and Excise when Branson failed to pay import tax on records brought in from overseas. He spent a night in jail and was fined £60,000, which he was allowed to pay back over three years. The case was not taken to court, but his family had to re-mortgage their home to help pay the costs. It gave the young businessman a wake up call that he wouldn't forget.

The rise and fall of Virgin Record Shops

1971 First Virgin Record Shop opens at 24 Oxford Street, London.

1979 Virgin Megastore opens at 14–16 Oxford Street in London. (The first time the term 'Megastore' was used.) Remains open until 2007.

1988 New Virgin Megastores open in Glasgow and Paris.

1990 First Virgin Megastore opens in Japan.

1992 First US Virgin Megastore opens on Sunset Boulevard in Los Angeles.

1996 Virgin Megastore opens in Times Square, New York City.

2000 First Megastore opens in the Middle East.

2000 Lagardere Group buy all French Megastores.

2002 Virgin Megastores launch in Australia.

2009 Virgin Megastores cease trading in the USA and Japan. Times Square branch closes in May.

Business Matters

$

Diversification

Companies often decide to offer new products or services — like Virgin expanding into travel, mobile phones and finance — because it reduces the risk of its other products becoming too limited or uninteresting. By adding new 'products' to its range, Virgin is providing extra reasons for customers to keep returning to the brand. When companies offer a completely different product or service, like Virgin expanding from a record label to transatlantic travel this is called 'brandstretching'.

Top of the pops

Entrepreneurs are not afraid of thinking big, and Richard Branson is no different. Not content with expanding his chain of record stores across the country, his next step was launching a Virgin record label.

In 1972, Branson took his involvement in the music business one step further by launching his own record label, Virgin Records. His cousin Simon Draper, who had been the buyer for the record stores and a key part of their success, became his right-hand man. Branson borrowed money from the bank and bought an Oxfordshire manor house, which he converted into a state-of-the-art recording studio called The Manor, where he also lived.

The Manor's recording facilities were rented out to new Virgin artists – including a teenage multi-instrumentalist called Mike Oldfield, who Simon and Richard spotted backing a singer who was recording there. Oldfield's debut album *Tubular Bells* (1973) was Virgin Records' first release and stayed in the UK charts for over five years!

Unlike many other small labels, Virgin decided not to license *Tubular Bells* to a larger, more powerful label, instead retaining the copyright and doing all the promotion themselves.

Multi-instrumentalist Mike Oldfield gave Virgin Records their first big hit with Tubular Bells.

Top of the pops: five of Virgin's best-selling albums

Spice by The Spice Girls, 1996, 28 million

No Jacket Required by Phil Collins, 1985, 25 million (released by Virgin in the UK and Ireland only)

Janet by Janet Jackson, 1993, 20 million

Tubular Bells by Mike Oldfield, 1973, 13 million

...But Seriously by Phil Collins, 1989, 11 million (released by Virgin in the UK and Ireland only)

> Virgin began to sign up new bands on the back of Mike Oldfield's success. The bulk of these would inevitably fail. We still paid ourselves tiny wages... and we reinvested all the money we earned in new artists and building up the company. **"**

Richard Branson, Losing My Virginity, 1998

Culture Club's worldwide success helped Virgin Records achieve huge profits in the early 1980s.

The album sold a million copies in the UK, and then was licensed to a US record label for a $1m advance (£620,000) and a large share of royalties. Virgin was making money fast.

Branson brought his sense of adventure to the music business, signing risky artists like the Sex Pistols in 1977, who had already been dropped by two record labels. In the year of the Silver Jubilee, Virgin released their single 'God Save The Queen', which sold over 100,000 copies in one week.

The Virgin label became the home of exciting new acts, including The Human League, Simple Minds, Heaven 17 and Culture Club – whose sales made a big contribution to Virgin's success. In 1982, Virgin made a £2m profit. By 1983 this had jumped to £11m, with 40% of that coming from Culture Club.

Brains

Behind The Brand

Trevor Key
Founder, Cooke Key Associates

Trevor was a graphic designer and photographer who created the iconic Virgin Group signature logo, which he first sketched on the back of a napkin!

With his partner Brian Cooke, Trevor founded Cooke Key Associates, a design agency. In total, Cooke Key produced over 150 album covers for Virgin and other record companies, including all Sex Pistols artwork and promotional material.
He died in 1995.

Making movies

Richard Branson never missed an opportunity for Virgin to grow and diversify. The next move was to open a film production and distribution company called Virgin Films.

Riding on the wave of the Sex Pistols' notoriety, Virgin Films invested £150,000 in a spoof documentary called *The Great Rock 'n' Roll Swindle*, which was filmed in 1978 and finally released in 1980.

The company also produced *The Space Movie* (1979), a NASA-backed documentary to celebrate the tenth anniversary of the *Apollo 11* moon landing, which also featured a soundtrack by Virgin artist, Mike Oldfield.

At the start of the 1980s, Virgin invested in an adaptation of a Graham Greene novel, *A Shocking Accident*, which won an Oscar for best short film. Encouraged by this success, in 1983 Virgin announced it would invest £14m in a series of films, including *Electric Dreams* (1984) and George Orwell's *Nineteen Eighty-Four* (1984), which featured a soundtrack from Virgin artists Eurythmics.

However, the unsuccessful *Absolute Beginners* (1986) struggled to earn back half of its £8.5m budget. Virgin decided to devote its time and resources to other parts of the brand, and closed down the movie production side of its business.

In 2010, 25 years later, Virgin Produced was founded as the film, television and entertainment division of the Virgin Group with a brief to develop, package and produce films and TV shows 'reflective of the Virgin brand'. Virgin Produced's first releases were *Limitless* (2011), starring Bradley Cooper and Robert De Niro; *Machine Gun*

Poster for The Space Movie *(1979) – with soundtrack by Virgin artist Mike Oldfield.*

Preacher (2011) starring Gerard Butler; and *Immortals* (2011), a 3D fantasy featuring Mickey Rourke. The three films contributed to worldwide box office sales of $400m (£250m).

Virgin Produced also invested in the 2012 worldwide hit *The Impossible* starring Ewan McGregor and Naomi Watts, and has releases planned for 2013 and onwards. If at first you don't succeed…

Nik Powell, who left the Virgin Group in 1983 to found film production company Palace Pictures.

Brains

Behind The Brand

Nik Powell
Co-founder of the Virgin Group

Nik was one of the co-founders of the Virgin Group with Richard Branson and Rob Stevenson, and Virgin Films in 1980.

In 1983 Nik left the Virgin Group to found Palace Pictures with film producer and director Stephen Woolley. The pair made some of the most well-known British films of the 1980s and 1990s, including *Mona Lisa* (1986), *The Crying Game* (1992) and *Interview with the Vampire* (1994).

Nik is currently director of the National Film and Television School in Beaconsfield, Buckinghamshire.

Business Matters

Forming a company

A 'limited' or 'incorporated' company — like many of the individual Virgin companies including Virgin Produced — is a business owned by shareholders (people who own shares in the company), and run by directors. The company's shares have a basic value, for example £1 each, which stays the same, and a market value, which goes up and down depending on how good an investment the shares are judged to be by people outside the company who want to buy them.

Taking to the skies

According to Richard Branson, his main motivation for constantly expanding into new ventures isn't money, but the challenge of trying to do something better than other people. He soon took on the biggest challenge of his life – Virgin Atlantic.

By 1983, Branson's Virgin empire included more than 50 companies with combined sales of over $17m (£10.5m). Nevertheless, when he launched Virgin Atlantic Airways in 1984, colleagues told him he was crazy to take on the established airlines, such as British Airways, who had already forced competitors into bankrupcy.

Branson strongly believed that the major airlines were not responding to their customers' needs, and was convinced that if he could create an airline that made travelling affordable and enjoyable, he could make Virgin Atlantic a success.

First reactions to Virgin Atlantic were brilliant. The airline became known for its superior service and well-equipped planes, including seat-back videos and free ice cream during films. But by the early 1990s, the global economy was weakening, the price of airline fuel had doubled, and fear of terrorist attacks meant fewer people were travelling abroad.

By 1992, Virgin Atlantic's financial situation was so poor that Branson was forced to sell his beloved Virgin Records to Thorn-EMI for $1 billion (£620m) to keep it afloat. The money allowed him to pay off the airline's debts and buy the company outright from his partners.

A Virgin Atlantic Boeing arrives in New York City – one of the airline's nine destinations in the USA.

> ❝ My interest in life comes from setting myself huge, apparently unachievable challenges and trying to rise above them. ❞

Richard Branson, Business Stripped Bare, 2008

Business Matters

$

Profit and loss

A profit and loss statement is a company's financial report that indicates how the revenue (money received from the sale of products and services before expenses are taken out, also known as the 'top line') is transformed into the net income (the result after all revenues and expenses have been accounted for, also known as the 'bottom line'). It shows the revenues for a specific period, and the cost and expenses charged against those revenues. The purpose of the profit and loss statement is to show company managers and investors whether the company made or lost money during the period being reported.

In 1999 the Virgin Group sold 49% of the airline to Singapore Airlines for £600m, retaining a majority 51% stake. In 2012, it was confirmed that Delta Air Lines in the USA would purchase Singapore Airlines' shares for £224m with plans to develop a transatlantic joint venture. Virgin Atlantic is determined to keep competing with the major airlines on its own terms.

Virgin Atlantic is still one of the highest profile companies in the Virgin Group. In 2012 the airline carried 5.4m passengers, making it the seventh largest airline in the UK. However, it is still not profitable and in 2013 made an operating loss of £70m, despite increased turnover and increased passenger numbers.

Craig Kreeger is confident that a partnership with Delta Airlines will benefit Virgin Atlantic.

Brains

Behind The Brand

Craig Kreeger
CEO, Virgin Atlantic

Craig joined Virgin Atlantic at the start of 2013 when former CEO Steve Ridgway retired. It's Craig job to maintain and grow the Virgin Atlantic brand, and oversee the new joint venture between Virgin and Delta Air Lines.

Craig is a graduate of the University of California in San Diego, with an MBA from UCLA (University of California, Los Angeles). He joined American Airlines in 1985, spending time in Europe, the Middle East and Africa, before being appointed Senior Vice President (Customer) in 2012.

Virgin keeps on growing

Richard Branson has developed a new business approach, which he calls 'branded venture capital'. He licenses the Virgin name to a new business – usually for a majority share – and wealthy partners supply the start-up cash. This has allowed Virgin to own or hold interests in more than 200 different companies. Here are just a few.

Virgin Active – a range of health clubs in the UK, South Africa, Australia and parts of Europe. **100% owned by Virgin.**

Virgin Cola – a soft drink launched in 1994 in conjunction with Canadian company, Cott. The US company closed in 2001, but the drink is still sold in several countries including France, Italy, Nigeria, China and Afghanistan. **100% owned by Virgin.**

The Spaceship Company – an aerospace production company that is building a fleet of commercial spaceships and launch aircraft with the aim of making widespread space travel a reality. **100% owned by Virgin.**

Virgin Books – a UK book publisher launched in the late 1970s. Specialises in adult fiction, business, health and lifestyle and celebrity biographies. **10% owned by Virgin (90% owned by publishing group Random House).**

London 2012 gold medallist Nicola Adams attends the launch of a Virgin Active club in London.

Business Matters

Company shareholders

Shareholders at companies like Virgin hope to make money in two ways. Firstly, as the company makes money, the value of its shares will rise, so an investor can make a profit if he or she sells their shares (known as a capital gain). Secondly, part of the profit that a company makes every year can be given to shareholders based on how many shares they own. This is called a dividend.

Virgin Trains holds the franchise to run the InterCity West Coast line until 2017.

> " You fail if you don't try. If you look at the history of American entrepreneurs, one thing I do know about them: an awful lot... have tried and failed in the past and gone on to great things. "

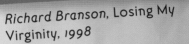

Richard Branson, Losing My Virginity, 1998

Virgin Money – a banking and financial brand, launched in the UK as Virgin Direct in 1995. Purchased Northern Rock in 2012. Currently has 4 million customers. **100% owned by Virgin.**

Virgin Trains – a UK train operating company that has operated the InterCity West Coast line since 1997. **51% owned by Virgin (49% owned by transport group Stagecoach).**

Virgin Mobile – a mobile phone operator launched in 1999, bought by NTL:Telewest in 2006. Now part of the EE network. **0% owned by Virgin.**

Necker Island – part of the British Virgin Islands, it was bought by Richard Branson in 1978 and turned into a luxury holiday resort for up to 28 guests. **100% owned by Virgin.**

Virgin Cosmetics – retailer and distributor of cosmetics founded in 1997. Renamed Vie at Home in 2006 to focus on direct selling of make-up, skin care, jewellery and homeware. **Sold by Virgin in 2009. Closed in 2011.**

Necker Island, bought by Branson for just £180,000 in 1978, and now part of the Virgin Limited Edition holiday portfolio.

Working at Virgin

According to Virgin boss Richard Branson, the success of the Virgin Group is built on its staff. So how does Virgin identify, hire and nurture the best people for its businesses?

> **"** If you take care of your employees, your employees will take care of your customers and your customers will take care of your shareholders. **"**
>
> Richard Branson, Business Stripped Bare, 2008

Flight attendants undergo six weeks of in-flight training before being passed to fly on Virgin Atlantic.

From hi-tech businesses like Google and YouTube, to service businesses like Virgin, employees can often make the difference between a company's success and failure. Whereas the brightest brains can give a hi-tech company the edge over its competitors by developing a radical new app or an advanced search algorithm, at companies like Virgin employees' skills might be overlooked.

The 'Virgin type' of person, according to Branson, 'enjoys working with others, is attentive, smiles freely, and is fun to be with. In business, someone who can stay cool and calm under pressure is an asset... Today's consumer can be very demanding, especially when things aren't going according to plan.'

Despite being a multinational business with thousands of employees, Virgin strives to recreate the atmosphere of Virgin's early years. Communication and the sharing of ideas between staff members are encouraged. Teams are kept small to aid this process.

'In the early days [of Virgin] when one of our companies... employed more than a hundred staff, we would split the company in two and promote the deputies to run the new company,' remembers Branson. Being the managing director of something small, rather than the assistant MD of something big, not only gives people more power, but requires them to acquire new skills, take pride in their success and learn from their failures.

Many Virgin businesses, including many of the airlines like Virgin Blue (Australia) and Virgin Nigeria, are independent companies with their own ownership structures. They therefore have the ability to make their co-owners rich by sharing in the company's success. Since the birth of Virgin, Branson estimates that over 100 employees have become millionaires or multimillionaires as a result of starting Virgin businesses!

Richard Branson at the launch of Virgin Australia in 2011.

Business Matters

Human Resources

The Human Resources (HR) department of a company is responsible for putting in place and maintaining the practices that allow effective management of staff. Some key responsibilities of an HR department are: 1) training; 2) staff appraisal: a formal process, performed by managers on their staff, which aims to assess how they are performing and to discuss what they need in order to improve and develop; 3) staff development: the processes in the company designed to identify the people with potential, keep them in the organisation, and move them into the right positions.

Virgin in your home

In 1996, Virgin launched its own Internet Service Provider (ISP) called Virgin.net. Today, Virgin is one of the biggest players in the lucrative UK mobile, broadband and television market.

Virgin Media was formed in 2006 after a merger between companies NTL, Telewest and Virgin Mobile UK. The deal created the UK's only 'quadruple-play' company, able to offer customers television, broadband internet, mobile phone and fixed phone lines, all under one roof. Virgin Media also owns and operates its own fibre-optic cable network, which is the only cable network in the UK.

In February 2007, the company was rebranded under the Virgin Media name, making it the largest Virgin company in the world. Overnight, Virgin Media had become the UK's most popular broadband provider, the largest mobile network and the second largest supplier of pay television and home phones.

Virgin Media owns and runs the only fibre-optic cable network in the UK.

The merger brought Virgin Media to the attention of Rupert Murdoch's British Sky Broadcasting (BSB), which became concerned that Virgin Media were also planning to buy a stake in ITV, Britain's largest commercial television channel. Worried that a combination of Virgin Media and ITV would prove serious competition to its own business, Murdoch's company bought 17.9% of ITV's shares at 135p per share for a total of £940m. Sky's part-ownership of ITV ended Virgin's interest in a share purchase.

> " True leadership must include the ability to distinguish between real and apparent danger. You need to understand the challenges to your enterprise and face up to them. Equally, you have to resist the temptation to overreact at the first sign of trouble. "
>
> Richard Branson; Business Stripped Bare, 2008

Sky also withdrew certain content from Virgin Media's television channels, losing itself a significant amount of advertising revenue (the money paid by companies to advertise their products during shows).

In retaliation, Virgin Media complained to the Office of Fair Trading, claiming that Sky's purchase of ITV shares had reduced competition in the UK television market.

The complaint was passed to the Competition Commission, who decided that Sky should reduce the number of their shares in ITV from 17.9% down to below 7.5%. Unfortunately for Sky, ITV's share prices had now fallen to just 40p each, meaning Sky lost £1.35 billion!

As of December 2012, Virgin Media has 4.8m customers, of which 3.8m subscribe to television services, 4.2m have broadband and 4.1m have phone services. The company's revenue of £4.1bn in 2012 provided a profit of £2.85bn, and continues to grow.

Richard Branson at the launch of Virgin Media in 2007.

Business Matters

Mergers and acquisitions

This phrase refers to the aspect of company strategy and finance that deals with the buying, selling and combining of different companies. This strategy can help a company grow rapidly within its market without having to create another separate company. An acquisition is the purchase of one company by another company. A merger is when two companies combine to form a

The height of ambition

Virgin Galactic is undoubtedly Virgin's most daring business launch to date. What could be more exciting than going into space?

Virgin Galactic was formed in 2004 to provide sub-orbital space flights to space tourists, sub-orbital launches for space science missions, and orbital launches of small satellites. It also aims to be able to provide orbital space flights in the future.

The spacecraft, *SpaceShipTwo*, is designed to launch from a special aeroplane, already in flight. *WhiteKnightTwo*, as is it known, carries the spacecraft to 16 km (52,000 ft). At this point, *SpaceShipTwo* ignites its own engines, reaching a speed of Mach 1.2 and a height of over 100 km (the Kármán line, where 'space' begins). Passengers will experience around six minutes of weightlessness, and can release themselves from their seats and float around the cabin.

Exciting for sure, and even better – there is already a great demand for the Virgin Galactic services. By early 2011, 400 people had signed up for the first flights, at a cost of $200,000 (£120,000) with a $20,000 (£12,000) deposit. By May 2013, prices had risen to $250,000 (£150,000) and there are currently around 650 people on the waiting list for the two-hour flights, including Professor Stephen Hawking, and actors Tom Hanks, Brad Pitt and Angelina Jolie.

Virgin Galactic astronaut Per Wimmer with a model of WhiteKnightTwo and SpaceShipTwo.

Initial flights are planned from Virgin Galactic's base in Las Cruces, New Mexico, with the service eventually expanding around the world. Virgin Galactic has also received valuable financial aid from the New Mexico authorities, who have invested around $200m (£121m) on a launch base, Spaceport America, including a 3,000 m (10,000 ft) runway and space-age terminal for travellers. Watch this space!

Business Matters

Research and development

Otherwise known as R&D, this is a business activity aimed at discovering solutions to problems or creating new goods and knowledge. R&D may result in ownership of intellectual property such as 'patents,' legal ownership of new products and the technology that produced them. For example, the Virgin Group also own The Spaceship Company (TSC), which manufactures *SpaceShipTwo* and *WhiteKnightTwo*.

George Whitesides joined Virgin Galactic from NASA to help launch Virgin's own space race!

Brains

Behind The Brand

George T. Whitesides
President and CEO of Virgin Galactic

As head of Virgin Galactic, George is responsible for overseeing all aspects of the company – from the construction of Virgin's fleet of commercial space vehicles to the operation of Spaceport America in New Mexico, USA.

Before joining Virgin Galactic in 2010, George served as NASA's Chief of Staff. When he left, George was awarded the Distinguished Service Medal, the highest award the agency offers.

George has a degree in Public and International Affairs from Princeton University, and an MPhil (Master of Philosophy) in Geographical Information Systems and Remote Sensing from Cambridge University in the UK.

Richard Branson – the adventurer!

Like Mark Zuckerberg at Facebook, Richard Branson has become the inescapable face of his brand. Branson's sense of adventure has kept the Virgin brand young and fun.

Just like his company, Richard Branson is always trying new things. Over the past 30 years he has broken several world records, and attempted many more – from the fastest Atlantic crossing to flying over the Arctic Circle in a hot air balloon!

Branson's first record attempt was in 1985, when he was asked to fund a catamaran that would attempt to win the Blue Riband trophy by crossing the Atlantic in the fastest recorded time.

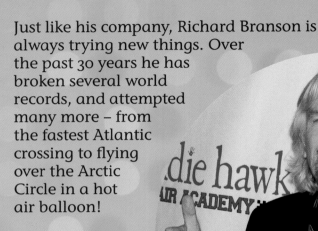

Virgin Atlantic had just launched and Branson believed a successful Atlantic crossing would generate huge publicity in both New York and London – the airline's only destinations at that time. The first attempt saw the Virgin Atlantic Challenger capsize and the crew rescued by the RAF. But the second attempt, in Virgin Atlantic Challenger II the following year, broke the existing record by two hours.

Branson at the Living Legends of Aviation awards in Los Angeles.

Branson didn't stop there. In 1987 his hot air balloon – Virgin Atlantic Flyer – successfully crossed the Atlantic. Then in January 1991, he crossed the Pacific from Japan to Canada, a distance of 10,800 km (6,700 miles), at a record-breaking speed of 394 km/h (245 mph).

Branson crossing the English Channel in an amphibious car in 2004.

Brains

Behind The Brand

Richard Branson
Chairman, Virgin Group

As Chairman of the Virgin Group, it's Branson's job to think strategically about how the group can grow and prosper. He takes an active role in staff recruitment, which he believes is the key to Virgin's continued success.

According the Forbes 2012 list of billionaires, Branson is the fourth richest citizen of the UK, with an estimated wealth of £2.9bn. In 2000 he was knighted for 'services to entrepreneurship', and in 2007 was included in the *Time Magazine* 'Top 100 Most Influential People in the World'.

In March 2004, Branson broke another record by crossing the English Channel in an amphibious vehicle in just 1 hour, 40 minutes and 6 seconds, beating the previous record by over four hours.

In 2008, however, Branson, with his family as crew, made an unsuccessful attempt at an eastbound Atlantic crossing in a 30 m (100 ft) yacht named Virgin Money. After two days, a monster wave seriously damaged the spinnaker, and severely ripped the mainsail, forcing the boat to return to harbour in Bermuda.

In the 2014 edition of the *Guinness Book of Records*, Richard Branson has three new entries – the oldest person to cross the English Channel by kiteboard, the richest presenter of reality television, and the most followers on social networking site LinkedIn. Branson is a born record-breaker!

Promoting the brand: Branson on camera

1991 Appears in *Only Fools And Horses*, as Del Boy gets on a Virgin Atlantic plane

1998 Appears in a London-based episode of US comedy *Friends* selling Union Jack hats outside Buckingham Palace

2004 Fronts a reality show on Fox in the USA *The Rebel Billionaire: Branson's Quest for the Best*

2004 Appears in the film *Around the World in 80 Days* – as a hot air balloon operator

2006 Appears in *Superman Returns*, credited as a 'Shuttle Engineer' alongside his son Sam

2006 Appears in *Casino Royale* at Miami airport – with Virgin Atlantic planes in the background!

A company with a conscience

Richard Branson is a long-time supporter of charitable causes, and often lends his time and resources to support everything from an end to nuclear weapons to the search for renewable energy sources.

In 2007, Branson, along with former US President Jimmy Carter, Archbishop Desmond Tutu and former Secretary-General of the United Nations Kofi Annan, were announced as founder members of a group called The Elders. The group, partly funded by Branson, would use their collective skills to try and end global conflicts, and promote green issues.

Perhaps not surprisingly for a man whose travel companies use vast energy resources, sustainability is a cause Branson feels very strong about. In 2007, he established the Virgin Green Fund to invest in projects targeting renewable energy in North America, Europe and emerging markets – projects that would not only benefit Virgin businesses but the whole world.

Branson at the launch of his 'Women on the move' programme at a Johannesburg University, funded by Virgin Unite.

Branson and son Sam, who is also an entrepreneur, as well as an investor in social media.

In March 2008 Branson hosted a gathering of some of the world's most influential politicians and businesspeople (including British Prime Minister Tony Blair, and Larry Page of Google) to discuss global warming-related problems.

Branson is a supporter of the Global Zero campaign, which works towards the worldwide elimination of nuclear weapons. He also established the Branson School of Entrepreneurship in South Africa in 2005, supporting new start-up businesses and providing mentoring and support to local entrepreneurs.

Virgin Unite, the charitable arm of the Virgin Group, was formed in 2004, and partners with more than a dozen charities worldwide to help raise funds for small charitable organisations focusing on AIDS research, child poverty and homelessness, and the eradication of malaria and tuberculosis in the third world.

> " There is such a thing as enlightened self-interest, and we should encourage it. It is possible to turn a profit while making the world a better place. "
>
> *Richard Branson, The Economist, 2010*

Brains

Behind The Brand

Shai Weiss
Founding partner of Virgin Green Fund

Shai was behind the formation of Virgin Green Fund, where he has been a partner since 2007. As a member of its Investment Committee, it's Shai's job to invest in renewable energy and resource efficiency projects that will benefit Virgin in the long term.

Before moving to Virgin, Shai held several management positions at NTL:Telewest. He was behind the merger with Virgin Mobile UK and the re-brand to Virgin Media. Prior to NTL, Shai ran the European office for the venture capital fund Jerusalem Venture Partners, and worked with bankers Morgan Stanley.

He has an MBA from Columbia University, and a degree in business and finance from City University in New York.

The future for Virgin

Business success is based on constantly moving forwards – adapting to change and reacting accordingly. Here's how we predict Virgin will change over the next few years.

In space

Virgin Galactic is a major investment in the future. With one spaceport due to open in New Mexico, and others planned around the world, the company could make huge profits by providing 'space travel' for the masses.

By owning the company that produces the spacecraft, Virgin can also benefit from other companies buying in tried-and-trusted Virgin technology, rather than spending billions of pounds developing vehicles themselves.

In the air

Virgin Atlantic's newly signed deal with Delta Airlines will massively increase Virgin's capacity to fly into and around the United States. The company is one of the most visible in the Virgin Group, but is far from the most profitable. Expect increases in Virgin Atlantic flights, customer numbers and – hopefully for Virgin – revenues over the next five to ten years.

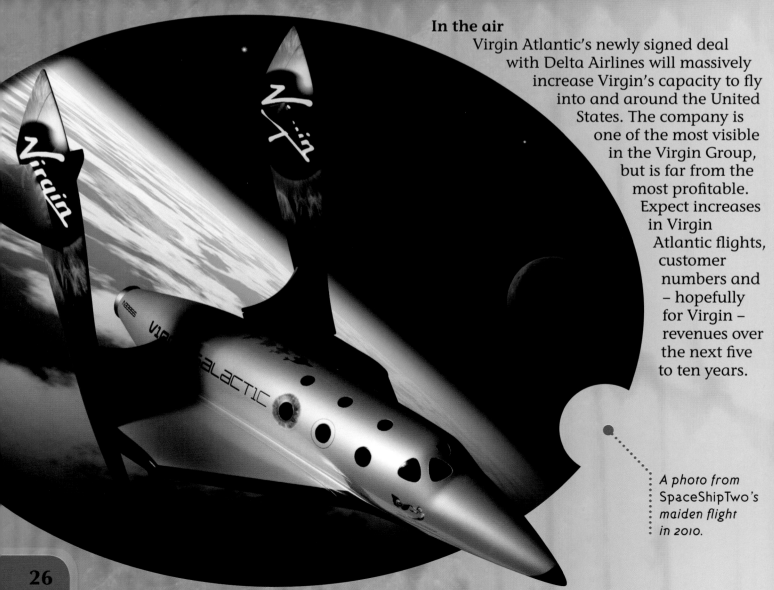

A photo from SpaceShipTwo's maiden flight in 2010.

In the home

Virgin Media is already one of the major players in the UK home entertainment market. We expect it to increase its output of self-produced TV shows, perhaps even launching a Netflix or Lovefilm.com-style subscription service. Virgin already has a background in film financing and production, so this would be a small but potentially lucrative step to take.

Out of the blue

Expect lots more adventurous projects from Virgin in the coming years. With Richard Branson's taste for adventure, and his love of adrenalin sports, it wouldn't be surprised to see Virgin launching its own Formula One team or backing a UK bid to bring the prestigious America's Cup yachting trophy back to Britain.

Brains
Behind The Brand

Josh Bayliss
CEO Virgin Group

As CEO of the Virgin Group, Josh is responsible for the management of the Group's capital investments and the overall Virgin brand.

Josh has been with Virgin since 2005, and became CEO in 2011. He has experience as a director of a large number of companies across the Virgin Group globally, in sectors ranging from aviation and travel, health and wellness, media/mobile, financial services and renewable energy.

Josh was previously a Senior Associate at leading international law firm Slaughter and May from 1999 to 2005. He holds a Bachelor of Laws and Bachelor of Arts from the University of Auckland, New Zealand.

Branson and daughter Holly with a Marussia Virgin Racing Formula One car. The team competed in the Constructor's Championship in 2010 and 2011.

Launch your own Virgin brand

To create a new product or brand, it is helpful to draw up a product development brief like the one below.

This is a sample brief for a new Virgin brand called Virgin Time Travel. The SWOT analysis on the page opposite will help you to think about the strengths, weaknesses, opportunities and threats for your brand. This can help you to see how feasible and practical your idea is before you think of investing time and money in it.

Product Development Brief

Name of brand: Virgin Time Travel

Type of company: Producing one-person 'travel pods' that allows users to travel backwards and forwards through time.

The brand explained (use 25 words or less):
Bored with the present? Why not experience the excitement of the past and the future with the unique Virgin Time Travel.

Target age of users: All ages (users must be 16 and over, and in good physical health. Doctor's note may be required.)

What does the brand do?: Virgin Time Travel manufactures 'travel pods' and sells the time travel experience to users worldwide.

Are there any similar products already available?: None

What makes your brand different?: Virgin Time Travel is a unique and groundbreaking company that allows users to travel in time. No other company is currently offering this service.

SWOT Analysis
(Strengths, Weaknesses, Opportunities and Threats)

Name of the Virgin brand you are assessing...
Virgin Time Travel

The table below will help you assess your Virgin brand. By addressing all four areas, you can make your product stronger and more likely to be a success.

Questions to consider

Does your brand do something unique?

Is there anything innovative about it?

What are its USPs (unique selling points)?

Why will people use this brand instead of a similar one?

Strengths

Virgin Time Travel is the only time travel company currently in the market.

Virgin Time Travel's 'travel pods' are comfortable, well designed and completely safe.

Why wouldn't people use this brand?

Can everyone use it?

Are there any dangers associated with the brand?

Do you have a help line/help desk in case people have problems with it?

Weaknesses

People afraid of changing the course of history may not want to use Virgin Time Travel.

Time travel puts the body under certain physical and emotional stresses, making it unsafe for the very young, the very old and the physically infirm.

In the event of a product malfunction, users may become trapped in the future or the past until they can be rescued.

Will the area that the brand serves become more important over time?

Can the brand be improved in the future, e.g. adapted for other uses?

Can it be used globally?

Can it develop new USPs?

Opportunities

It is envisage that as prices to time travel fall, families may use Virgin Time Travel instead of traditional holiday destinations.

Multi-person 'travel pods' will be produced, to send groups of people through time together.

'Themed' travel experiences will be offered – visits to the Roman Colosseum, the 1966 World Cup Final for English football fans, and so on.

Is the market that you are selling into shrinking?

Will it face competition from other brands?

Will new legislation make the brand illegal?

Are any of your weaknesses so bad they might affect the brand in the long run?

Threats

There is a danger of people sueing Virgin Time Travel if they are injured using the product.

Inevitably, other companies will join the market with their own version of time travel.

Governments may rule against the brand if there are circumstances where time travel alters the course of history.

29

Do you have what it takes to work at Virgin?
Try this quiz!

1) What's your favourite subject at school?

a) PE. Oh, and I quite like food tech because we can eat what we make.

b) English. I enjoy creative writing and letting my imagination run wild.

c) Maths. Numbers make the world go round!

2) What do you want to do when you leave school?

a) I'm not thinking about that yet. I'm just looking forward to half-term.

b) I want to go to university and hopefully get a good job in an office.

c) I'm going to start my own business. I've got lots of great ideas.

3) You're given a pencil and paper, and asked to create something new. Do you:

a) Write your name in bubble writing.

b) Draw a very accurate portrait of the person sitting next to you.

c) Make a plan for a new product or service that you think customers will love.

4) Who is your favourite businessman?

a) Does the Prime Minister count?

b) Alan Sugar. I love it when he says, 'You're fired!'

c) Richard Branson. He doesn't stand still, and is always planning something new.

5) Name one business you wish you had thought of first.

a) Krispy Kreme doughnuts. Think of all the freebies!

b) Facebook. I'd be a gazillionaire by now.

c) The business I want to do hasn't been launched yet. Want me to let you into a secret?

6) If you could launch your own business, what would it be?

a) Mmm, come back to me when I've finished watching this TV programme.

b) I love clothes, so I would probably open a clothes shop

c) Glad you asked! I've been doing some research into what customers want in my area. Shall I show you the findings?

7) If you were asked to come up with a new company for the Virgin Group, would you say:

a) The Virgin Group? Were they at Glastonbury this year?

b) Gosh, they've done so much already, I wouldn't know where to start.

c) I think what's missing from the Virgin portfolio is a groundbreaking smartphone.

Results

Mostly As: Sorry, but your chance of working at Virgin is looking shaky! It doesn't sound like you have much interest in business to succeed at this world-famous company.

Mostly Bs: You're aware of business, but you need to give it more time and attention if you want to succeed in a very competitive business.

Mostly Cs: Congratulations, it sounds like you have what it takes to succeed at the Virgin Group. Keep working hard at school, and pushing to be the best, and who knows?

Glossary

adaptation a film or play, for example, that has been made from a book

amphibious vehicle a vehicle that can operate both on land or in water

bankruptcy a situation where a person or company becomes unable to pay their debts

buy a stake buy shares in a company

capsize to turn upside down by accident while on water

catamaran a boat with two parallel hulls. Its broader base is designed to make it more stable

chairman a person who is in charge of a large company

copyright the legal right that someone has to control the production and sales of something, for example recorded music

diversify to produce a range of different types of products or services in order to succeed in more markets or protect against risk

dyslexia a difficulty with reading and writing caused by the brain being unable to see the difference between some letter shapes

emerging markets markets that are just beginning to exist

entrepreneurial a term used to describe someone who makes money by starting their own business, especially when it involves spotting a new opportunity and taking risks

eradication the removal or destruction of something harmful or dangerous

fibre-optic cable a very thin glass or plastic thread through which light can travel to carry information

imported made in one country and brought into another in order to sell it

joint venture a business or business activity that two or more people or companies work on together

licensed produced and sold with the permission of the company who created it

MBA Master of Business Administration. An advanced degree in business

mentoring supporting and advising someone with less experience to help them develop in their work

merger a situation in which two or more companies join together

notoriety the state of being famous for something bad

orbital space flights that leave the earth's atmosphere and do a complete orbit of the planet

rebranded if a company rebrands, it creates a new name or image for itself, often to try and change the way that people think about it

renewable energy energy that is produced by the sun, wind etc rather than using fuels such as oil or coal

spinnaker a special type of large sail, used to catch the wind from a specific angle

sub-orbital space flights that leave the earth's atmosphere but do not complete a full orbit of the planet

sustainability the idea that goods or services should be produced in ways that do not use resources that cannot be replaced, and that do not damage the environment

virgin a person with no experience of a particular activity

Index

BIG BU$INE$$

Contents of titles in this series:

More titles in the Big Business series

WAYLAND